BEYOND THE PAYCHECK

BUILDING EMPOWERED, FULFILLED, AND THRIVING TEAMS

BY

VERONICA WILLIAMS

Dedication

To my loving family, whose unwavering support has been my foundation, and to my incredible husband, your encouragement, patience, and belief in my dreams have made this journey possible.

To my mentors, thank you for seeing potential in me, for challenging me to grow, and for modelling the very leadership this book is about.

This work is for you and for everyone striving to lead with purpose, empower others, and create a lasting impact.

- Veronica Williams

Background & Inspiration

This book was born from a lifelong curiosity about human nature. From an early age, I found myself deeply intrigued by how people think, what motivates them, and how they grow. That curiosity guided me to pursue a bachelor's degree in psychology—an academic journey that gave me language, structure, and theory for the insights I had been gathering all along. It really opened my eyes to the idea that behind every behaviour, a story that wants to be heard.

Over time, I transitioned from being a student to a leader.

Taking on leadership roles has been an eye-opening experience. I have seen how a caring, self-aware, and empathetic leader can positively influence not just the success of a business but also the lives of the people involved. It has become clear to me that leadership is not about holding authority—it is about serving others, inspiring change, and guiding with responsibility.

Whether through coaching, mentoring, or simply sharing what I have learned with others, I have found deep purpose in helping people reach their full potential. From conversations over coffee, coaching calls, and collaborative team reflections, small but powerful spheres of influence emerged.

Over time, I noticed a pattern that people truly thrive when they feel seen, valued, and purposefully aligned with the work they do.

Beyond the Paycheck captures that journey. It is for anyone who leads people, those who aspire to lead, and the people who believe that work can be about more than just earning a paycheck. It aims to inspire and be a driving force for empowerment, purpose, and growth.

Introduction

Why This Book Matters Now?

We are experiencing a quiet revolution in the workplace. Gone are the days when a paycheck was sufficient. Today's employees are asking more meaningful questions.

Does this work matter? Do I belong here? Am I growing?

In boardrooms and break rooms alike, people seek more than pay; they crave connection, purpose, and the opportunity to thrive.

As a leader, I have observed this shift unfold firsthand. I have seen talented individuals disengage when they felt overlooked, and I have witnessed individuals come alive when their strengths aligned with meaningful work. I have learned that empowerment is not a luxury; it is a leadership duty. When employees feel valued, trusted, and recognized, they not only perform well but also thrive, and this is what this book is about.

This book is about understanding what truly motivates people — starting with basic human needs — and creating an environment where they can bring their whole selves to work. It is about shifting from outdated leadership models that prioritize control to ones that foster trust, autonomy, and growth.

You will notice that this book combines psychology, leadership strategies, and personal reflection. That is intentional.

My academic background in psychology has given me a language for understanding human behaviour; my professional experience in leadership and coaching has provided practical insights into what works and what does not. Additionally, my passion for people, their development, dreams, and dignity unite them all.

Beyond the Paycheck is more than just a guide for people managers. It is for anyone who aims to lead intentionally, inspire excellence, and build organizations where people do more than survive. It is about supporting employees to flourish by growing, contributing meaningfully, while feeling valued for who they are and what they bring.

Welcome to a different kind of leadership.

Let us get to work.

- Veronica Williams

Contents

Chapter 1
Understanding Maslow's Hierarchy of Needs

Maslow's Hierarchy of Needs - A foundational model for human motivation.

Figure 1. Maslow's Hierarchy of Needs (Maslow, 1943).

At the core of human motivation lies a simple yet profound truth: *people are driven by their needs.*

This understanding is central to creating workplaces where employees can thrive. One of the most enduring frameworks for understanding this is Maslow's Hierarchy of Needs.

The Five Levels of Human Needs

Maslow's model suggests that people are motivated by five levels of needs, which build upon one another:

1. Physiological Needs

These are the basic survival needs: food, water, and rest. In a workplace context, this translates to fair wages, reasonable working hours, and a safe and comfortable work environment.

2. Safety Needs

Once basic needs are met, individuals seek safety, job security, benefits, and a predictable work environment.

3. Love and Belonging

Humans are social beings. We crave connection, inclusion, and a sense of belonging. Teams that foster collaboration, support, and inclusion meet this need.

4. Esteem

This level includes self-respect and recognition from others. Positive feedback, promotions, and being valued for contributions all fulfill esteem needs.

5. Self-Actualization

At the top is the desire to grow, reach one’s full potential, and do meaningful work. This is where people feel truly fulfilled.

Workplaces and the Hierarchy

Understanding where your employees fall on this hierarchy can transform how you lead them. An employee struggling with job insecurity ***(Level 2)*** will not be able to focus on creative innovation ***(Level 5***). Conversely, when all five levels are addressed, employees become energized, innovative, and deeply committed to their work.

Why This Model Still Matters

We are in an era where retention, engagement, and employee well-being are paramount. Maslow's framework reminds us that people bring their whole selves to work. When leaders help meet these human needs, the workplace becomes more than a job; it becomes a platform for growth and fulfillment.

Real-World Examples

From Enthusiastic to Disengaged - What Changed?

Sarah is a recent graduate, thrilled to start her first job as a customer support associate. Initially, the job satisfies her physiological, safety, and belonging needs, but as time passes and development opportunities remain limited, Sarah becomes disengaged.

What Could Help Sarah Thrive?

1. Provide a Development Plan:

Sit down with Sarah to understand her goals. Create a clear growth roadmap that includes skill-building opportunities or job shadowing.

2. Offer Stretch Assignments:

Assign her to a cross-functional project or let her lead a training session. These small acts build esteem and open the door to self-actualization.

3. ***Recognize Strengths Publicly:***

Celebrate her contributions in team meetings or highlight her success in newsletters. This boosts esteem and encourages continued growth.

4. Ask for Input & Ideas:

Involve her in decision-making processes or customer service improvements. This signals that her voice matters—meeting esteem and belonging needs.

The Leadership Lesson:

Early enthusiasm diminishes when growth stalls. When you invest in an employee's development, they not only stay longer but also engage more fully.

Real-World Example 2: The Doctor Who Stopped Feeling Seen

Daniel is a qualified doctor who, due to immigration restrictions, now works in a warehouse to support his family. At first, he is grateful for the job, but gradually starts to feel overlooked and unfulfilled. His sense of identity and purpose slowly diminishes, impacting his well-being and work performance.

What Could Help Daniel Thrive?

1. Acknowledge His Story:

Take time to listen. Recognize his background with empathy, not as overqualification, but as untapped potential.

2. Create Purposeful Roles:

Could Daniel train new employees? Translate safety protocols into multiple languages? Help mentor others? Use his experience meaningfully.

3. Support Educational Pathways:

Offer tuition support or flexible schedules if he is seeking certification. Connect him with programs or mentors in his field of interest.

4. Connect Him with a Mentor or Peer Group:

Pair him with someone who has been through a similar transition. Create a sense of community and belonging through shared experiences. Be careful with this strategy because if the person is not entirely healed, this can create trauma bonding and have an adverse effect.

The Leadership Lesson:

Unseen talent is wasted talent. When leaders create space for someone's whole story, they do not just retain a worker; they restore a dream.

Personal note: I have met many Daniels throughout my career in Canada, and at one point, I was one myself. What helped during difficult moments was knowing the work I was doing made a difference. Whether it was a certificate of recognition or a letter from a client telling me how I impacted their lives, these kept me motivated to give my best while continuing to find ways to help.

Optimal Outcomes: What Happens When Leaders Get It Right

Sarah:

When her manager developed a plan and recognized her contributions, Sarah's passion for the role reignited. Within a year, she moved into a team lead position and began mentoring new hires. Her voice was valued, and she found purpose in helping others grow, moving steadily toward self-actualization.

Daniel:

His supervisor took the time to learn about his background and offered him a role in training new staff and translating safety materials. The company connected him with an internal mentor who had also requalified in a new country. Feeling seen and supported, Daniel enrolled in a certification program with flexible shifts that allowed him to attend classes on his schedule. His confidence returned, along with his sense of identity and purpose.

Conclusion:

The Extra Step That Changes Everything

Leadership is not only about achieving goals or overseeing performance. It is about fostering environments where everyone feels valued, supported, and encouraged to grow and reach their full potential.

The stories in this chapter show what happens when needs are fulfilled and what happens when they are not. Sarah lost momentum not because she lacked ability, but because of the uncertainty around her; her path forward was unclear. Daniel did not lose value when he changed countries; he lost visibility. Both were willing, capable, and full of potential; however, both needed leaders who could see beyond the surface. When leaders take that extra step to ask more questions, to recognize hidden potential, to align work with purpose, they move from managing to truly empowering.

Furthermore, when employees feel empowered, the ripple effects are undeniable:

- Engagement rises
- Innovation increases
- Retention improves
- Trust deepens
- Culture strengthens

Supporting people holistically is not a *soft* strategy; it is a powerful one. It is how organizations build loyalty, resilience, and long-term success. When people feel fulfilled, they not only do more work but also produce their best work.

Leaders play an important role in shaping this experience. When they foster environments of trust, empathy, and recognition, employees feel empowered to bring their whole selves to work. They are more likely to engage, innovate, and stay committed.

This is not just a feel-good idea; it is backed by research. Gallup's 2022 report found that engaged employees are 21% more productive and 59% less likely to look for a new job (Gallup, 2022).

Deloitte's Human Capital Trends report echoes this, emphasizing that organizations with strong cultures of belonging outperform their peers (Deloitte, 2021).

Creating a healthy workplace does not happen by accident. It takes up intentional effort. It requires leadership, clear values, and a commitment to listening. Thriving workplaces begin when leaders take action.

The human side of work involves recognising that people are more than just workers; they are whole individuals with dreams, challenges, and potential. When organisations embrace this truth, they unlock a deeper level of engagement and loyalty.

In the chapters ahead, we will explore how leaders can cultivate positive cultures that foster well-being, promote genuine connections, and inspire meaningful impact.

Chapter 2
Matching Strengths to Roles
The Power of Alignment

Before leaders can assign people to the right roles, they must understand what each team member brings to the table. This is more than just what is on their résumé. It is who they are at their best.

Beyond the Résumé: Why Deeper Understanding Matters

A résumé tells you what someone *has done*.

However, it rarely reveals:

- What energizes them

- How they handle pressure
- What kind of environment helps them thrive
- Their hidden talents or passions
- Their values and motivations

To assign people to the right roles, leaders need to dig deeper into who someone is at their best. That involves understanding not just skills, but strengths, personality, and purpose.

Leadership today demands more than strategic thinking. It requires emotional intelligence, empathy, and the ability to truly listen and understand. In a world where employees are navigating uncertainty, burnout, and rapid change, leaders who show up with compassion and curiosity make all the difference.

Listening is not passive. It is an active and intentional practice that fosters trust and psychological safety. When leaders take time to understand their team's experiences, concerns, and aspirations, they create space for honest dialogue and meaningful connection. This listening fosters a sense of belonging, which in turn drives performance.

Brené Brown reminds us that vulnerability is not weakness; it is the foundation of courageous leadership (Brown, 2018). Leaders who are willing to admit what they do not know, ask for feedback, and share their own challenges model authenticity. That authenticity invites others to do the same.

Organizations that prioritize emotional intelligence notice measurable benefits. Teams with emotionally intelligent leaders report higher engagement, lower turnover, and stronger collaboration. Suitable for the company and the people.

According to a study by TalentSmart, emotional intelligence accounts for 58% of performance in all types of jobs, and 90% of top performers have high EQ (TalentSmart, 2020).

Emotional intelligence is not just about being nice; it is about being effective. It means recognizing when someone is struggling, navigating conflict effectively, and responding with empathy rather than defensiveness. It is about creating a culture where people feel safe to speak up, take risks, and grow.

Listening also means being open to change. When employees share feedback, ideas, or concerns, leaders must be willing to act on changes if required. That responsiveness shows respect and builds credibility. In the workplace, it forms the foundation for trust, engagement, and transformation. Leaders who listen do not just manage, they inspire.

It tells people, *"We listen. Your voice matters here."*

In a noisy world, listening is a superpower.

What can leaders do?

1. Observe behaviour in action:

Watch what excites people. What tasks do they volunteer for? When are they most energized? When do they lose track of time? Strengths often reveal where effort feels natural and performance is smooth, even if the task is complex. Have you ever worked through your lunch without noticing? That is the natural effort you want to see in your staff.

2. Ask the right questions and use open-ended prompts like:

"What do you love doing even if you are not doing it at work?"

"What have you felt most proud of in your achievements?"

"If you could design your ideal workday, what would be in it?"

This allows talking and learning more about the staff.

3. Use strength-based tools:

Tools like Clifton Strengths[1] can be used to confirm what leaders observe and foster deeper discussions about development and role fit.

4. Review Past Achievements:

Looking beyond job titles, hobbies, volunteer work, and informal leadership activities, all these aspects build your skills and character, and can reveal clues to someone's natural talents.

5. Invite Peer Feedback:

Encourage staff to ask colleagues:

"When have you seen me at my best?" or "What do you rely on me for?"

Others often notice what we ask colleagues:

"When have you seen me at my best?" or "What do you rely on me for?"

Others often notice what we miss. Too often, we assign people roles based on availability, urgency, or convenience rather than alignment with their strengths, interests, and potential. When a person's natural talents and passions align

---

[1] Clifton Strengths® is a psychometric tool that measures people's personality and thought processes (Collins, 2022; Hair et al.).

with their work, it truly makes a difference: they feel more energized, focused, and dedicated.

Why Alignment Matters?

People want to feel useful, not just have a job and be employed. The world has moved on from that now.

When someone's job aligns with their strengths, they feel:

1. More confident
2. Capable
3. Engaged
4. Self-motivated
5. Loyal to the organization
6. Creative
7. Solution-oriented

One of the most overlooked causes of disengagement in the workplace is not laziness or a lack of talent, but rather misalignment. Matching strengths to roles fulfils core psychological needs: esteem, belonging, and self-actualization.

See some tips and tricks to get you started:

1. **Assess Strengths Early:** Utilize strengths, tools, and engage in meaningful conversations during onboarding and check-ins.

2. **Tailor Responsibilities When Possible:** Minor role tweaks can boost engagement. Let a strong communicator run a team meeting or assign a detail-oriented person a documentation project.

3. **Encourage Job Crafting:** Allow employees to have a say in how they work. Autonomy can be as powerful as recognition.

4. **Create a Talent Inventory:** Maintain a list of hidden or emerging strengths within your team. This can help guide assignments and succession planning.

Organizational Benefits of Strength Alignment - Fewer performance issues - Higher retention - Faster onboarding and development - Increased innovation and morale.

When people feel confident that they are in the right role on the right bus, they drive the mission forward more quickly and with more joy.

Building Relationships Through Ongoing Dialogue

Matching an employee to the right role is not a one-time task. It is a continuous process rooted in genuine connection. Leaders should engage in regular, informal conversations with team members beyond traditional performance reviews and appraisals. These check-ins foster trust and help leaders understand their team's evolving strengths, interests, and challenges.

When leaders truly understand their people, they can advocate more effectively, assign meaningful projects, and prevent disengagement. Relationship-driven leadership creates psychological safety, where employees feel recognized, heard, and supported.

A well-timed chat can reveal a hidden skill, a brewing frustration, or a fresh idea. These moments help build stronger connections and create a more resilient, innovative team.

Real-World Examples

The Overlooked Leader

Monica was an administrative assistant known for her reliability and calm presence. What her supervisor did not realize was that Monica had successfully led several nonprofit fundraisers in her community. During a casual check-in, Monica shared this part of her life. Recognizing her leadership and coordination skills, her manager asked her to organize the company's wellness month initiative. Monica exceeded expectations, and within a year, she moved into a project coordinator role by aligning her job with her strengths.

The Miscast Analyst

David was hired as a data analyst, but over time, it became clear that the work drained him. He dreaded spending hours with spreadsheets. However, he often brightened when explaining data trends during meetings or training new team members. His manager reassessed his strengths and redefined David's role to include internal presentations and onboarding sessions. He was not just retained. He became a key link between analytics and operations, bridging a gap the company had not even recognized.

The Leadership Takeaway:

Sometimes, the key to unlocking performance is not coaching someone harder but finding a better fit. When strengths are matched with opportunity, engagement and effectiveness naturally increase.

The Leadership Lesson

Hidden potential stays hidden until someone takes the time to look for it. When leaders intentionally align people's strengths with their roles, they do more than fill a position—they unlock purpose.

Personal note: Throughout my career, I have seen the difference alignment makes. Early on, I worked with an employee whose volunteer experience revealed leadership potential her résumé never captured. That discovery transformed her confidence and career trajectory. It reminded me that when leaders take time to learn *who* people are—not just what they do—they open doors that might never have been seen.

Optimal Outcomes: What Happens When Leaders Get It Right

Monica

After her leader recognized her fundraising background, Monica's strengths came alive. Her coordination and communication skills flourished, leading to advancement and renewed confidence.

David

When David's manager realigned his role to match his presentation strengths, his enthusiasm returned. Collaboration improved, and his impact multiplied—proof that engagement follows alignment.

Conclusion: The Alignment Advantage

Matching strengths to roles is not just efficient—it is transformational. When people use their best qualities daily, they experience energy, ownership, and purpose.

Alignment shifts the workplace from obligation to contribution. The ripple effects are undeniable:

- **Engagement increases** because work feels meaningful.
- **Confidence grows** because success feels natural.
- **Retention improves** because employees feel valued.
- **Innovation flourishes** because diverse strengths are leveraged.
- **Culture strengthens** because collaboration replaces competition.

Research supports what human experience already proves. Gallup finds that employees who use their strengths daily are **6 times more likely to be engaged** and **3 times more likely to report excellent quality of life** (Gallup, 2022). Harvard Business Review adds that strength-based organizations see **up to 19% higher sales and 29% higher profits** (HBR, 2021).

Alignment does not happen by chance; it takes curiosity, courage, and consistent conversation. It begins when leaders look beyond job descriptions to see the *person* behind the position.

The human side of leadership recognizes that people are not interchangeable; they are individuals with stories, talents, and dreams waiting for the right fit. When leaders create that fit, performance becomes personal, and purpose becomes possible.

In the chapters ahead, we will explore how leaders can build upon this foundation—shifting from alignment to advancement by creating opportunities for continued growth, recognition, and development.

Chapter 3
Empowerment in Action — Creating Ownership and Growth

From Alignment to Empowerment

In Chapter 2, we emphasized the importance of recognizing employee strengths and matching them with suitable roles. But the journey does not stop once someone finds the right position. For people to truly thrive, they need to feel empowered—meaning they should have the freedom, support, and responsibilities to grow within their roles and beyond.

Empowerment involves giving people a sense of ownership over their work and responsibilities. It entails trusting them to make decisions, try out new ideas, and learn from both successes and failures. When employees feel empowered, they become more engaged, resourceful, and dedicated to their goals and the organisation's mission.

What Empowerment Looks Like

True empowerment is about more than handing off tasks. It involves:

- Clarity: Clearly defined expectations and outcomes
- Autonomy: The ability to decide how to achieve those outcomes
- Support: Coaching, encouragement, and resources
- Accountability: Ownership of results and learning from them

Why Empowerment Matters

When leaders empower employees, they fulfill key psychological needs:

1. Autonomy: Feeling trusted and in control
2. Mastery: Developing competence and confidence
3. Purpose: Connecting personal goals to organizational impact

Empowered employees are:

1. More engaged
2. More innovative
3. Better problem solvers
4. More resilient to change

They not only do what is asked, but they also take initiative, improve systems, and inspire others to do the same.

Common Barriers to Empowerment

Despite its benefits, many organizations unintentionally block empowerment.

Common obstacles include:

1. Micromanagement: Leaders who check every detail stifle creativity and trust
2. Unclear expectations: Employees cannot own results they do not understand
3. Fear-based cultures: If mistakes are punished, risks will not be taken
4. Siloed leadership: Lack of cross-department trust or communication

Overcoming these requires a mindset shift: from control to coaching, from directing to developing.

Empowerment Through Relationship

As highlighted in Chapter 2, you cannot empower those you do not know.

To assign someone to the right role and later empower them to take ownership, leaders must forge genuine relationships. This means:

1. Having regular check-ins beyond performance reviews
2. Creating space for employees to share their aspirations and challenges
3. Understanding how personal and professional goals connect
4. Recognizing and celebrating progress—not just outcomes

Empowerment is personal. Each employee has their own unique way of thriving. Some flourish with independence, while others benefit from regular feedback and reassurance. Understanding these relationships helps us discover what kind of support and empowerment suits each person best.

Real-World Examples

The Empowered Frontline Worker

Maria was a retail associate known for being helpful and attentive. One day, she told her manager that many customers appeared confused by the store layout. Instead of dismissing her, her manager advised her to submit a proposal for improvements. She did, and her ideas were excellent yet simple.

The store adopted her suggestions, leading to higher customer satisfaction scores. Maria was later promoted to store trainer. She not only enhanced the customer experience, but she also became an advocate for change and a role model for her peers.

Maria's story illustrates that empowerment does not always begin at the top; it often starts when a leader listens. Encouragement turned a helpful employee into a change agent, mentor, and role model for others.

The Manager Who Let Go

Jacob was a middle manager known for doing everything himself. His team relied on him for every decision, which slowed progress and caused burnout. When a new director encouraged him to delegate and develop his team's skills, Jacob was hesitant but willing to give it a try.

Jacob began with small projects, guiding team members to make decisions rather than making them for them. Over time, his team grew more confident and proactive. Eventually, one team member assumed a leadership role, enabling Jacob to focus on higher-level strategic projects with renewed energy.

When Jacob let go, his team stepped up.

What Leaders Can Do to Empower Teams

1. **Start with Strengths**

Refer to Chapter 2. Empowerment begins with matching the person to the right work.

2. **Set Clear Goals, Not Just Tasks**

Focus on desired outcomes. Let employees shape the process.

3. **Coach, Do Not Command**

Ask guiding questions instead of providing all the answers.

4. **Encourage Smart Risk-Taking**

Normalize failure as part of growth. Reward effort and learning, not just success.

5. Build Psychological Safety

Create space where employees feel safe sharing concerns, feedback, and ideas.

6. Provide Growth Paths

Offer training, mentoring, and new responsibilities regularly. Not just at promotion time.

The Return on Investment of Empowerment

Organizations that prioritize empowerment experience:

1. Greater innovation and process enhancements
2. Increased staff retention and job satisfaction
3. Stronger internal leadership pipelines
4. A culture of accountability and initiative

The Leadership Lesson

Empowerment thrives where trust replaces control. When leaders give people ownership, they invite them to think, create, and lead. Empowerment is not losing authority—it's multiplying it.

When people feel a sense of ownership, they not only work harder but also work smarter and care more deeply about their work. Empowerment is not a reward; it is a strategy.

Personal Note: Early in my leadership journey, I learned that empowerment often begins with a single conversation. I once worked with a team member who hesitated to share ideas, convinced that her input would not matter. When I invited her to co-lead a project and supported her decisions, she flourished. Her confidence grew, and so did her contributions. That experience taught me that leadership is not about holding power—it is about sharing it.

Optimal Outcomes: What Happens When Leaders Get It Right

Maria

Empowerment transformed Maria from a helpful associate into a leader. Maria's initiative improved customer experiences, strengthened the team's sense of ownership, and created a ripple effect of positive change throughout the store.

Jacob

By stepping back, Jacob allowed his team to step forward. Delegation led to development. His employees became more capable, confident, and collaborative, while Jacob rediscovered purpose in leading strategically rather than operationally.

Conclusion: The Empowerment Advantage

Empowerment is not a soft concept—it's a performance strategy. It turns compliance into commitment and transforms workplaces from dependent to dynamic. When leaders understand their people, align strengths, and create space for growth, they don't just develop teams—they cultivate future leaders.

The ripple effects are profound:

- Innovation accelerates because people feel trusted to experiment.
- Engagement deepens because work feels meaningful.
- Retention strengthens because employees feel valued.
- Leadership multiplies because empowered people empower others.

According to Gallup (2022), employees who feel empowered are 67% more engaged and 23% more likely to innovate in their roles. Deloitte's Human Capital Trends report reinforces this, showing that organizations with empowerment cultures experience significantly higher performance and satisfaction (Deloitte, 2021).

Empowerment is not about letting go—it is about lifting. It is the bridge between potential and performance, and the hallmark of leaders who lead with trust, courage, and vision. Empowerment transforms a workplace from a dependent to a dynamic one. When leaders know their people, match them to the right roles, and create growth opportunities, they build a stronger team and also develop the next generation of leaders.

In the next chapter, we will explore how leaders can sustain empowerment through recognition, continuous feedback, and growth pathways that keep engagement alive long after the initial spark.

Chapter 4
Thriving Workplaces: From Survival to Sustainable Success

Why Thriving Matters More Than Engagement

For years, organizations have measured workplace health through satisfaction and engagement. Satisfaction ensures that foundational needs—fair pay, safety, and stability—are met. Engagement reflects emotional investment and alignment with organizational goals.

But in today's rapidly changing, burnout-prone world, even engaged employees can feel depleted.

Thriving goes further. It is a state where people experience both vitality (energy, enthusiasm, and purpose) and learning (growth, mastery, and development). According to Gretchen Spreitzer and Christine Porath (2012), thriving employees are 16% more productive, 32% more committed, and 46% more satisfied with their jobs.

Thriving is not a perk—it is a performance strategy. It is when people feel fully alive at work.

From Surviving to Thriving: What is the Difference?

Survival is reactive. Thriving is intentional.

Thriving cultures feel human. People feel safe, valued, and challenged to grow. They do not require large budgets, but they do require leadership to be consistent, empathetic, and attentive to detail.

Maslow's Hierarchy in Action

When we revisit Maslow's Hierarchy of Needs, genuine thriving happens once higher levels (belonging, esteem, and self-actualization) come into focus.

After an employee's basic needs for salary, safety, and security are met, they seek connection, purpose, and growth. A thriving workplace nurtures these higher needs through inclusive recognition and opportunities for self-development.

Thriving is not a "program." It is a culture created by what people experience every day—how leaders listen during challenges, how they respond to mistakes, and how often they share credit. The daily choices leaders make determine whether people simply survive or truly thrive.

The Three Pillars of Thriving

1. Emotional Well-Being — Safety, Belonging, and Recognition

Thriving begins with emotional safety—the confidence to express ideas, ask questions, and admit mistakes without fear of embarrassment or punishment. When employees feel heard, respected, and appreciated, they engage more deeply.

Research & Insights:

Harvard's Amy Edmondson (1999) demonstrated that psychologically safe teams outperform others in innovation and learning. Bhoir & Sinha (2024) confirmed that HR systems built on empathy and emotional support are essential for long-term well-being.

Practical Tools:

- *Case Study: Recognition Huddles: Five-minute weekly rituals to celebrate small wins.*

- *Thriving Check-Ins: Ask, "What part of your work gives you energy?" or "What is feeling heavy this week?"*
- *Belonging Builders: Encourage peer appreciation and team storytelling.*

Turning Around a Team in Decline

A mid-sized nonprofit struggled with morale. Employees felt overworked, disconnected, and unsure of how their work contributed to the mission.

A new director began not by launching new strategies but by listening—meeting every employee and asking:

- "What is working?"
- "What is frustrating you?"
- "What would make your work more meaningful?"

She implemented simple yet powerful changes: weekly progress updates that connect daily work to impact, flexible schedules, and peer appreciation moments. Within six months, performance and morale improved dramatically. The team rediscovered meaning because their leader chose understanding over directives.

Five Behaviors That Foster a Thriving Culture:

1. **Lead with Purpose:** Connect individual work to the larger mission.
2. **Listen Like It Matters:** Seek to understand before offering solutions.
3. **Recognize More Than Results:** Celebrate learning and effort, not just outcomes.
4. **Make Learning Visible:** Share lessons and growth stories openly.
5. **Put People Before Process:** Adapt systems to serve people, not the other way around.

2. Mental Well-Being — Resilience, Autonomy, and Rest

Thriving requires emotional energy and mental stamina. Leaders who build resilience into the workplace—through autonomy, flexibility, and clarity—help employees handle change and recover from stress more easily.

Research & Insights:

REBA (2023) identifies mental well-being as one of the top three predictors of performance and retention. A *Future Business Journal* (2024) review highlights the post-pandemic urgency for mental health systems that strengthen resilience and adaptability.

Practical Tools:

- **Energy Audits:** Track tasks for a week and label them as Energizing, Neutral, or Draining. Adjust workloads accordingly.
- **Resilience Coaching:** Offer access to professional or peer-led sessions on stress management.
- **Autonomy Agreements:** Empower employees to shape *how* they reach outcomes, not just *what* they achieve.

Consulting Firm Reclaiming Energy

A mid-sized consulting firm offered great pay but was losing people fast. Exit interviews revealed the same story: *"I am exhausted but not challenged."*

Leaders piloted energy audits, project swaps, and resilience coaching. Within months, **turnover dropped 18%**, innovation surged, and engagement rose 22%. The key was not time off; it was redesigning work around purpose and energy.

3. Professional Well-Being — Growth, Mastery, and Meaning

Professional thriving happens when employees see a future for themselves. It is not only about promotions—it is about learning, expanding, and connecting daily work to personal growth.

Research & Insights:

Kevin Burns (2024) found that professional development drives retention, while Gallup's studies show employees who see growth opportunities are twice as likely to stay.

Practical Tools:

Team Thriving Map: Record each person's strengths and learning goals; align them with new projects.

Role-to-Purpose Exercise: Ask, "How does your work improve someone else's day?"

Learning Showcases: Create space for team members to share new skills or insights.

Thriving Nurses Amid Shortages

Amid severe staffing shortages, a hospital unit created peer-support circles, recognition huddles, and skill-rotation programs. Within a year, patient satisfaction rose 15%, sick days declined, and morale rebounded. Small acts of connection and empowerment rebuilt trust and energy.

When Leaders Get It Right

When leaders embrace the principles of thriving, the results ripple across teams and organizations:

- **The Nonprofit Director:** By listening first and acting with empathy, she transformed a disengaged workforce into a connected, purpose-driven community. The organization not only met its goals but also reignited its mission through trust and collaboration.
- **The Consulting Firm Executives:** When they stopped treating burnout as a personal weakness and started viewing energy as a leadership responsibility, employees rediscovered creativity and ownership. The culture shifted from exhaustion to innovation.
- **The Hospital Leaders:** By investing in peer support and skill rotation, they reminded their nurses that their growth mattered as much as their output. The result was not just retention—it was renewed pride in the profession itself.

In each story, thriving did not come from policy—it came from **presence**. From leaders who chose connection over control, trust over fear, and curiosity over assumption. These leaders did not just manage—they empowered, listened, and lifted.

Thriving happens one courageous leadership choice at a time.

The Power of Belonging

Belonging is the soil from which thriving grows. When people feel valued for who they are, not just what they do, they contribute to their best selves. They collaborate more, innovate freely, and form communities of support that outlast any single initiative.

Thriving Teams Are Resilient Teams

Teams that thrive are better equipped for change. They respond to stress with creativity, not collapse. They share responsibility, trust each other's intentions, and move forward together.

Bringing the Pillars Together

Emotional safety encourages people to speak up. Mental resilience provides them with the strength to persist, while professional growth gives them a sense of purpose to stay.

Together, these pillars create a culture of vitality, a living system where innovation and humanity coexist. Kim Cameron's research in Positive Organizational Scholarship confirms that thriving organizations outperform their peers in creativity, collaboration, and adaptability. When leaders nurture the whole person, the organisation itself becomes stronger, steadier, and more human.

Personal Note: Early in my leadership journey, I managed a team that was performing well but feeling drained. Instead of immediately setting new goals, I paused and asked, "What part of your work brings you joy?" What would make it meaningful again? Their answers led to small, human-centered changes—recognition check-ins, peer mentoring, and flexible project ownership. Within weeks, energy returned.

That experience taught me this truth: people rarely burn out from hard work—they burn out when their effort feels unseen or disconnected from purpose. Thriving begins the moment we see the whole person, not just the performer.

Leadership Takeaways

Thriving begins with listening: Ask what energizes or drains your team.

Anchor culture in safety and belonging: People cannot grow where they do not feel safe.

Focus on energy, not just efficiency: Sustainable performance requires rest and reflection.

Connect every role to purpose: Meaning fuels motivation.

Recognize progress often: Consistent appreciation builds trust and loyalty.

Invest in development: Growth conversations and mentorship sustain engagement.

Lead with humanity: Care, transparency, and consistency transform workplaces into thriving communities.

Conclusion

Thriving workplaces are built—not by policies or perks—but by people who lead with intention and empathy. They are cultivated through small, consistent actions that show employees they are seen, supported, and trusted.

When organizations move beyond survival, they unlock the higher levels of human potential—belonging, esteem, and self-actualization—just as Maslow envisioned. The outcome is a culture where innovation, well-being, and purpose coexist in balance.

Leaders who prioritize thriving do not just create happier teams; they create healthier, stronger, and more sustainable organizations. They turn workplaces into communities of growth, and performance into purpose.

Thriving is not accidental; it is intentional, and it begins with leaders who have the courage to care.

Chapter 5
Recognition and Growth — The Dual Engines of Engagement

Beyond Bonuses: What People Really Want

Many leaders still equate recognition with rewards — raises, plaques, or "Employee of the Month" titles. While fair pay is essential, it is not what makes people care. What truly drives engagement is the feeling of being seen, valued, and appreciated for one's unique effort.

Recognition says, "I see you. What you do matters." When employees receive this kind of affirmation, they feel a sense of belonging. They stop working for validation and start contributing from pride.

Recognition is not a gesture — it is communication. It tells people that they are more than their job descriptions. It transforms workplaces from transactional to transformational.

The Science of Recognition

According to Gallup, employees who receive regular recognition are four times more engaged and five times more likely to feel connected to their organization's culture. Deloitte's research echoes this: when recognition is frequent and sincere, productivity rises and turnover drops.

Neuroscience explains why — recognition releases dopamine, the brain's "feel-good" chemical. It reinforces desired behaviors while creating emotional safety and trust.

Recognition is not an afterthought; it is a leadership strategy.

The Principles of Meaningful Recognition

Gallup, Deloitte, and SHRM all confirm that regular recognition increases engagement, motivation, and retention. But to be meaningful, it must be:

- **Genuine:** Authentic and specific — not routine or forced.

- **Timely:** Delivered close to the moment of achievement.
- **Balanced:** Celebrating both effort and outcomes.
- **Inclusive:** Ensuring all contributions, big and small, are seen.

Recognition triggers dopamine, the "feel-good" chemical, which reinforces positive behavior and strengthens trust. But beyond biology, it creates something far more lasting: a sense of emotional safety and purpose.

Types of Recognition That Work

Public Praise: Acknowledge achievements in meetings or newsletters.

Private Appreciation: A heartfelt thank-you note or personal message.

Tangible Rewards: Extra time off, lunch, or small tokens of appreciation.

Opportunities to Shine: New projects or leadership assignments.

Peer Recognition: Encouraging colleagues to celebrate one another.

 *The Quiet Achiever*

Sarah, an IT analyst, quietly prevented a system failure that could have halted operations. Her leader learned about it from a colleague and publicly recognized her contribution.

The ripple effect was immediate: team morale lifted, collaboration strengthened, and "thank-you" became a common phrase.

Recognition turned invisibility into empowerment, and it spread.

Growth Is Not a Ladder. It Is a Map.

Growth today isn't about climbing a corporate ladder. It's about movement — learning, experimenting, and finding purpose. Employees want to know that their role grows with them, not beyond them.

Growth includes:

- Cross-functional/lateral skill development
- Mentorship and coaching
- Certifications and workshops

The modern leader's question is:

- "Is this role growing with this person — or is this person outgrowing their role?"

Leaders as Development Partners

The best leaders are not just managers; they are *development partners.* They coach, guide, listen, and help employees connect aspirations to opportunity. In other words, they help employees discover their potential.

Ask thoughtful questions like:

"What excites you right now?"

"Where do you want to grow?"

"How can I support your next step?"

Growth becomes sustainable when leaders ask — and then act.

The Crossroads

James, a customer service representative, showed leadership potential. Everyone assumed he would move into management. But during a one-on-one, James admitted he preferred teaching to supervising.

Instead of forcing him upward, his leader created a new role in training and onboarding. James flourished, eventually leading company-wide learning initiatives.

He did not climb the ladder; he redrew the map.

When Leaders Get It Right

When leaders see both the person and the potential:

- Sarah found visibility through recognition when her leader built up confidence through recognition
- James found growth through understanding when his leader built up loyalty through listening and personalized growth.

Recognition builds energy. Growth channels it.

Personal Note: Early in my career, I worked with a family, mainly with the caregiver, to apply for disability benefits. At the end of the case, the caregiver brought me flowers and a handwritten note.

"You have handled every challenge with grace. Thank you for being so persistent. It matters."

It was not tied to a bonus or a review — just humanity. That note became my reminder that recognition does not have to be big to be powerful.

Now, when I recognize others, I aim to make it personal and specific — because I know how one moment of being seen can change how someone sees themselves.

Leadership Takeaways

Recognition fuels engagement: growth sustains it. Praise effort, not just outcomes.

Creating learning visibility makes growth part of the culture. Recognition without development fades; development without recognition frustrates. Ensure to be:

- Be specific, sincere, and timely when showing appreciation.
- Growth is not a promotion — it is progress.
- Recognition without development feels hollow; development without recognition feels thankless.

Leaders who combine both build loyal, purpose-driven teams.

Conclusion: Recognition and Growth Are Strategic, Not Optional

Recognition fills the emotional bank account. Growth builds the future. Together, they meet two of humanity's greatest needs — to be seen and to become.

When leaders recognize effort, they build confidence. When they nurture growth, they build capacity. When both coexist, employees stop working for validation and start working from inspiration.

Recognition lights the spark. Growth keeps it burning. Together, they form the foundation for what comes next — listening, the skill that transforms connection into trust. When people feel valued for who they are *and* supported in who they are becoming, engagement is no longer something you measure; it is something you feel. That is when leadership evolves from management to mentorship — and from supervision to significance.

Chapter 6
Leadership That Listens —
The Feedback Loop of Trust

Listening as Leadership

Leadership is not about having the answers; it is about creating space for them to emerge. When leaders listen deeply, they transform meetings into meaning and make data into dialogue.

Listening is how people feel safe, valued, and understood enough to speak. It is how respect becomes reciprocal. And it is how authentic leadership begins.

The Listening Deficit

Many leaders believe they are listening, but they are often waiting to talk. Reports and dashboards reveal performance, not pulse. The result is disengagement disguised as agreement.

The World Health Organization and Gallup both note that disengagement costs the global economy over $8 trillion annually. The cure is not more direction, it's more dialogue.

Why Listening Is a Leadership Superpower

Listening builds trust, accelerates problem-solving, and strengthens creativity. It:

- Validates experiences
- Surfaces hidden challenges early
- Encourages ownership and innovation

Listening says, "You belong here, your voice matters."

Five Practices of a Listening Leader

1. Create Safe Spaces. People speak when they feel safe.
2. Ask Open Questions

"What's working?"

"What is draining you?"

4. Listen to Understand, Not Reply: Stay present and curious.

Follow Through.

5. Listening without action breeds frustration.
6. Normalize Feedback Loops: Make dialogue a habit, not a special event.

Listening That Transformed Retention

A retail district manager faced high turnover and low morale. Instead of launching new policies, she visited every store and asked one question:

What would make this a place you want to stay?"

She listened without defending or interrupting — then acted on simple feedback. Within six months, turnover dropped 30%, and engagement soared.

Listening, not policy, transformed the culture.

When Leaders Get It Right

Listening leaders earn trust before they need it.

The retail manager restored connection with one question.

The executive who practiced silent reflection discovered solutions that no meeting could produce.

Listening builds commitment one conversation at a time.

Personal Note: Years ago, I led a team through a major organizational change. One morning, a quiet, reliable employee resigned unexpectedly. When I asked why, she said softly,

"I just don't think anyone's been listening."

That sentence changed me.

I realized I'd been speaking at my team, not with them. I started holding weekly "listening sessions" with no agenda, no PowerPoints, just space. Within weeks, people began sharing openly again.

That experience taught me that leadership isn't about having the loudest voice. It's about creating room for others to use theirs.

Leadership Takeaways

- Listening is empathy in action.
- Ask before assuming.
- Notice silence — it often speaks loudest.
- Close the loop; show what changed because you listened.

Conclusion: Listening Is the Foundation of Everything

Listening isn't a pause in leadership — it is leadership. It's how trust begins, how innovation takes root, and how belonging is built.

When leaders listen with presence and curiosity, they discover the stories behind the statistics and the person behind the performance.

Listening turns direction into dialogue and dialogue into trust. It's through this trust that teams find the courage to bring their full selves to work.

Chapter 7
Trust at the Core — The Outcome of Empathy and Consistency

The Currency of Leadership

Trust is the invisible currency that sustains leadership. It cannot be demanded — it must be demonstrated. When trust exists, teams take initiative. When it erodes, even high performers disengage. Trust is what turns leadership from authority into influence.

Why Trust Outlasts Perks

Perks attract, but trust retains.

Research shows employees in high-trust cultures experience (Great Place to Work, n.d.).:

[2]74% less stress

50% higher productivity

76% more engagement

40% less burnout

People do not leave organizations; they leave environments where trust has thinned.

The Three Dimensions of Trust

1. **Competence — Can You Deliver?** Reliability and clarity build confidence.
2. **Character — Do You Do What's Right?** Integrity means fairness even when it's inconvenient.
3. **Care — Do You Have My Best Interest in Mind?** Compassion creates loyalty no policy can buy.

Building Trust in Practice

- Share why, not just what.
- Keep promises, even small ones.

---

[2] (Deloitte Digital, 2023). Deloitte Digital. (2023). *Workforce experience by design: Building trust and connection in the modern workplace.* https://www.deloittedigital.com/us/en/insights/perspective/workforce-experience-by-design.html

- Admit mistakes quickly and learn publicly.
- Invite honest dialogue.
- Recognize fairly and consistently.
- Invest in growth as a signal of faith in potential.

A Culture Shift Through Trust

A tech company's engagement scores were sinking despite good pay and perks. The new CEO started sharing quarterly financial updates, including the struggles. Managers began hosting "connection conversations."

Within 18 months:

Turnover dropped 25%

Engagement rose 30%

Three innovations emerged from employee ideas

Transparency did not weaken authority — it built it.

When Leaders Get It Right

- The CEO earned credibility through honesty.
- Managers rebuilt confidence with consistency.
- Employees responded with creativity and loyalty.
- Trust is the quiet engine behind every thriving culture.

Personal Note: Once, I made a well-intended decision without explaining it. The next day, tension filled the room. Finally, someone said, "We would have understood if you had just told us why."

That moment humbled me. I acted responsibly but not transparently. I called a meeting, explained my reasoning, and apologized. That honesty rebuilt more trust than perfection ever could.

It reminded me that trust grows in the soil of honesty, and sometimes the most powerful leadership moment is saying, "You are right, I should have handled that differently."

Leadership Takeaways

- Trust is built, not assumed.
- Transparency is strength, not weakness.
- Care before control.
- Integrity is remembered long after outcomes are forgotten.

Conclusion: The Human Equation of Leadership

Trust is the thread that ties everything together. It's built when leaders consistently recognize, listen, and lead with integrity.

Recognition sparks connection: It helps people feel seen. *Listening builds understanding:* It helps people feel heard. *Trust completes the cycle:* It helps people feel safe.

Together, they create cultures that thrive in workplaces where people show up not because they must, but because they want to. When leaders lead with empathy, honesty, and follow-through, they stop managing tasks and start cultivating beliefs.

A culture rooted in trust doesn't fear mistakes; it learns from them. It doesn't avoid change — it adapts through it. And it doesn't rely on one strong leader — it multiplies leadership across every level. Recognition opens the heart. Listening opens the mind. Trust opens the future. That is the accurate measure of leadership, not authority, but impact.

Chapter 8
Purpose, Meaning, and Fulfillment at Work

Why Purpose Matters More Than Perks

Today, as burnout, disengagement, and quiet quitting become more common, many employees find themselves asking deeper questions about their work and what truly gives their life purpose.

- "Does my work truly matter?"

- "Am I making a real difference?"

- "Is this job just a paycheck, or part of something significant?"

Purpose is like the heart of our work, turning everyday tasks into something meaningful. While perks might catch people's attention initially, it is the sense of purpose that truly keeps them motivated and committed.

According to a 2020 McKinsey report, nearly 70% of employees find their sense of purpose through their work. When people see how their roles connect to a bigger mission, they tend to be more motivated, resilient, and loyal, even when things get tough.

Understanding the Psychology of Purpose

Purpose in the workplace is not just an abstract concept; it has a real psychological impact. Viktor Frankl, in his classic work *Man's Search for Meaning*, emphasized that those with a strong "why" can endure almost any "how." This perspective translates into several workplace benefits:

- Enhanced perseverance in stressful situations.

- Boosted creativity and initiative.

- Stronger emotional ties to the organization.

Research by Yale's Amy Wrzesniewski reveals that when people see their work as a calling, rather than just a job, they often feel more satisfied and perform better. Cultivating a sense of purpose is not just for nonprofit organizations; it can flourish in any environment.

Two Pathways to Purpose

1. Job Crafting

Job crafting gives employees the chance to personalize their roles, making them more aligned with what they're good at, passionate about, and truly value. This empowers them to find more satisfaction and purpose in their work.

It includes:

- Task crafting: Changing what you do

- Relational crafting: Changing who you interact with

- Cognitive crafting: Changing how you think about your work

Wrzesniewski and Dutton's research indicates that job crafting results in higher engagement, lower burnout, and a stronger sense of identity at work.

2. Narrative Building

Narrative building helps employees reframe their contributions within a larger story. It is the difference between "I clean floors" and "I create a safe healing environment."

When leaders reinforce these narratives, employees feel seen, respected, and essential.

Case Study 1: The Hospital Janitor

At a children's hospital, a janitor described his role not as cleaning, but as "creating a safe space for healing." Leadership embraced this narrative by:

- Publicly recognizing janitors during staff meetings.
- Including them in patient care briefings.
- Sharing stories of their impact on families.

Results:

- Morale improved across departments.
- Interdepartmental respect increased.
- Turnover among support staff dropped by 12%.

Applied Tools:

Role-to-Purpose Exercise:

- "How does your work improve someone else's day?"
- "What would happen if your role disappeared?"
- "What is one part of your work that feels most meaningful?"

Retail Associates and Storytelling

A national retail chain faced high turnover among frontline staff. Employees felt disconnected from the brand's mission and undervalued in their roles.

Leadership responded by:

- Reframing associates as "customer experience ambassadors".

- Offering storytelling workshops to help staff articulate their impact.

- Recognizing moments of delight created by employees.

Results:

- Customer satisfaction scores rose 18%.

- Attrition dropped 22%.

- Employees reported higher pride in their work.

Applied Tools:

- Narrative Building Workshops

- Recognition Beyond Results: Celebrating creativity, empathy, and alignment with values—not just sales metrics

- Interactive Tool: Purpose Pulse

Use this quick reflection tool in team meetings or surveys:

- “What part of your work feels most meaningful?”

- “When was the last time you felt proud of your contribution?”

- “How does your role connect to our mission?”

These questions help leaders surface hidden sources of fulfillment and identify gaps where purpose may be lacking.

Creating Purpose-Driven Workplaces

Organizations that embed purpose into their culture share three standard practices:

1. Transparent Communication

Regularly team efforts to the broader mission. Share stories of impact, customer feedback, and strategic goals.

2. Recognition Beyond Results

Celebrating effort, creativity, and values alignment—not just performance metrics.

3. Opportunities for Impact

Invite employees into decisions that affect them. Please give them a voice in shaping policies, projects, and priorities.

Supporting Research:

Gallup’s 2023 State of the Global Workplace report found that employees who feel their opinions count are 4x more likely to be engaged.

Kevin Burns (2024) emphasizes that purpose-driven cultures outperform others in retention, innovation, and resilience.

Leadership Takeaway

Purpose is not just a luxury. It is an important part of leadership. When employees recognize themselves not just as workers, but as important contributors to a larger story, they tend to be more resilient, innovative, and loyal. This mindset helps create a more engaged and motivated team, fostering a sense of shared purpose that benefits everyone.

Leaders who cultivate purpose unlock:

- Emotional commitment

- Discretionary effort

- Cultural transformation

Conclusion: Purpose as the Anchor of Fulfillment

Purpose is the quiet power that keeps people steady through change. Perks may attract talent, but *purpose keeps hearts engaged.*

When people understand how their work matters — how it touches others, strengthens the mission, or shapes something larger than themselves — they find energy that no incentive can replicate.

Leaders who cultivate purpose do not just manage performance; they ignite passion. They remind people that their roles are not just about *tasks*, but about *transformation*. When employees find meaning in what they do, they bring their whole selves to work, creative, resilient, and proud.

As Viktor Frankl taught us: “Life is never made unbearable by circumstances, but only by lack of meaning and purpose.”

When leaders connect people to their “why,” they help them not just survive work but *thrive* in it.

Chapter 9
Building Systems That Support Fulfillment

Why Systems Matter

Culture is often described as “how things are done around here.” Every cultural norm is really supported by a system—comprising policies, practices, and structures—that can either help us flourish or hold us back. While inspiring leaders can spark change, it is the systems they create that keep the momentum going and ensure lasting success.

Many organizations depend heavily on heroic leadership to boost engagement, but when those leaders move on, the energy tends to dwindle. To truly succeed, fulfillment should become a natural part of the organization's core, woven into systems that encourage flexibility, well-being, growth, and inclusion. This approach creates a more resilient and supportive environment for everyone.

As organizational psychologist Adam Grant notes, "The strongest cultures are not built on charisma—they are built on consistency."

Three Systemic Foundations of Fulfillment

1. Flexibility and Autonomy

Rigid schedules and one-size-fits-all policies are now outdated remnants of the industrial era. Nowadays, more and more people in the workforce truly appreciate autonomy, adaptability, and being trusted to do their best.

Key Practices:

- Remote and hybrid work options.

- Flexible hours and compressed workweeks.

- Autonomy in task execution and decision-making.

Supporting Research:

A 2023 Deloitte study found that flexible work arrangements are the top driver of employee well-being and retention.

Gallup reports that employees with high autonomy are 43% more likely to be engaged.

Practical Tools:

Flexibility Framework: Create clear guidelines for remote work, flexible hours, and asynchronous collaboration.

Autonomy Audit: Ask teams, "Where do you feel trusted to make decisions?" and "Where do you feel micromanaged?"

2. Well-Being and Resilience Support

Well-being is not just about perks—it is about designing work that does not deplete people. Organizations must move from reactive wellness programs to proactive system design.

Key Practices:

- Mental health days and wellness stipends.
- On-demand counseling and peer support networks.
- Workload management and recovery rituals.

Supporting Research:

REBA's 2023 report identifies mental well-being as one of the three pillars of employee success. The World Health Organization classifies burnout as an occupational phenomenon, rendering it a systemic issue rather than a personal one.

Practical Tools:

Resilience Toolkit: Offer resources like mindfulness apps, coaching sessions, and recovery planning.

Wellness Integration Checklist:

- Are rest and recovery built into our workflow?

- Do employees feel safe discussing mental health?

- Are workloads regularly reviewed for sustainability?

3. Growth, Recognition, and Inclusion

Fulfillment flourishes when people feel seen, stretched, and supported. Systems must reward not just performance, but also effort, creativity, and alignment with values.

Key Practices:

- Career development stipends and peer coaching

- Inclusive leadership training and mentorship circles

- Recognition platforms that celebrate diverse contributions

Supporting Research:

Kevin Burns (2024) emphasizes that inclusive, growth-oriented systems outperform others in innovation and retention. McKinsey's 2022 report shows that organizations with inclusive cultures are 35% more likely to outperform financially.

Practical Tools:

Recognition Playbook: Train managers to use a 3-step model:

Name the contribution.

Explain its impact.

Link it to company values.

Inclusive Leadership Checklist:

Have I asked every voice for input?

Did I recognize diverse contributions today?

Have I challenged my own assumptions?

Tech Startup Retention Strategy

A fast-growing startup faced mass attrition and declining morale. Leadership realized that perks were not enough—they needed systemic change.

They introduced:

- Flexible schedules and remote-first policies
- Peer recognition platforms tied to company values
- Personal development stipends for coaching and courses

Results:

- Turnover dropped 40%.

- Employee satisfaction scores rose 30%.

- Internal promotions increased by 25%.

Applied Tools:

- Flexibility Framework.

- Recognition Playbook.

- Growth Stipends.

Manufacturing Plant Inclusivity

A manufacturing plant struggled to promote gender inclusivity and retain employees from underrepresented groups. Leadership responded by:

Launching bias training and inclusive leadership workshops

Creating mentorship circles for women and minority employees

Adjusting shift policies to be more family-friendly

Results:

- Productivity rose 12%.

- Engagement scores improved across demographics.

- Applications from diverse candidates increased by 40%.

Applied Tools:

- Inclusive Leadership Checklist

- Mentorship Circles

- Family-Friendly Scheduling

- Thriving in the Workplace: Insights and Practices

Key Highlights:

- Voluntary turnover decreased by 18%.

- Internal innovation surged, resulting in two new client acquisitions.

- Employee engagement scores improved by 22%.

Approaches We Used:

- Conducted an Energy Audit Exercise to redesign roles.

- Implemented Resilience Coaching to promote mental well-being.

- Organized Project Swaps to align employees' tasks with their passions.

Leadership Insight:

Thriving is not just a state of mind; it is a tangible measure of growth and energy. Leaders who focus on more than just keeping employees satisfied — those who actively design for a thriving environment — unlock hidden potential.

Characteristics of Thriving Employees:

- They tend to stay longer.
- They drive innovation.
- They contribute positively to the workplace culture.

Research by Kim Cameron on Positive Organizational Scholarship reveals that thriving cultures consistently outperform others in terms of creativity, collaboration, and resilience.

Chapter 10
Self-Awareness and Growth as a Leader

"Transformation begins with self-awareness." — Veronica Williams.

Why Self-Awareness Matters

Strong leadership does not begin with strategy, authority, or technical skill. It begins with knowing yourself.

Self-awareness is the practice of understanding:

- how you show up,
- how you are perceived,

- and how your presence affects the people around you.

Without self-awareness, even well-intended leaders can create harm — micromanage out of fear, ignore issues out of avoidance, or shut down voices without realizing it. With self-awareness, those same leaders become intentional, grounded, and trusted.

This is where real transformation begins.

The Foundation of Emotional Intelligence

Emotional is more than being "nice" or "supportive." It is a core leadership competency.

Daniel Goleman (1995) describes emotional intelligence as five interconnected capacities:

1. **Self-awareness** – I understand my emotions and triggers.
2. **Self-regulation** – I can manage my state instead of letting it manage me.
3. **Motivation** – I am driven by purpose, not ego.
4. **Empathy** – I can interpret and honor what others are feeling.
5. **Social skill** – I can build trust, navigate tension, and move people toward a shared goal.

Leaders who grow in these areas create psychological safety, inspire loyalty, and influence without force. They do not just direct work — they elevate the people doing it.

Recognizing Your Impact

Leadership is not neutral. Your mood, tone, energy, and urgency are constantly being read and absorbed by your team. Kahn (1990) notes that team climate and performance often mirror the leader's emotional posture. In other words, people will often match you.

- If you are frantic, they become anxious.
- If you are withdrawn, they become guarded.
- If you are steady, they can breathe.
- If you are clear and honest, they feel safe to be clear and honest with you.

This is why self-awareness is not optional. You are always setting the room's temperature, even when you do not mean to.

Ask yourself, daily:

- “What did people feel when I walked in today?”
- “Did I create tension or calm?”

- “Did I invite voices, or did I shut people down without realizing it?”

That level of reflection is not self-criticism. It is leadership hygiene.

Case Study: The Anxious Manager

Maria led a capable, experienced team — and yet everything had to go through her. Every email. Every client update. Every decision. She called it “quality control.” Her team called it micromanagement.

Underneath her behavior was anxiety.

She was afraid that if anything went wrong, it would reflect on her — so she tried to control every detail. What she could not see at first was the impact:

- her team stopped making decisions,
- work slowed down,
- morale fell,
- and she was burning herself out in the process.

Through coaching, Maria began to recognize her pattern. She was not “protecting the work.” She was protecting her fear.

We worked on two simple shifts:

1. Naming the emotion instead of acting it out ("I am nervous about this deliverable" instead of silently taking it over).
2. Handing over decisions with clarity, not panic ("You own this. I am here if you need me.").

Within six months:

- Her team started operating with more autonomy.
- She reduced her involvement in low-risk decisions.
- Delivery performance improved by 15%.
- Her team reported feeling "trusted rather than watched."

Her team did not change first. She did.

That is the quiet power of self-awareness: when a leader shifts, the system responds.

Continuous Leadership Development

Self-awareness is not "one breakthrough moment." It is a practice.

Leaders who keep growing tend to build deliberate habits around their development. Some of the most effective tools include:

- **Coaching:** Creates a safe space to explore patterns, blind spots, and pressure points without judgment.
- **Mentorship:** Offers lived wisdom and perspective from someone who has navigated similar challenges.
- **Peer feedback:** Gives you honest insight into how you are showing up right now — not how you think you are showing up.
- **Reflection journaling:** Helps you see trends in your own reactions and leadership behavior over time.
- **Pause-and-check moments:** Before a tough meeting, ask yourself, "What energy am I walking in with, and is it the energy this room needs?"

These are not signs of insecurity. These are signs of maturity.

Leaders who seek feedback and self-correction are often the most trusted, because they model what they ask from others: openness, humility, and growth.

The Leadership Mirror (Leader Tool)

Here is a simple, practical tool you can start using immediately.

Step 1: Ask three people you work with — not just friends, but people who have seen you under pressure — two questions:

- "What do I do that helps you do your best work?"
- "What do I do that makes it harder?"

Listen. Do not explain. Do not defend. Just thank them.

Step 2: End each day with this reflection:

- "How did my presence affect the team's energy today?"
- "If everyone behaved the way I did today, would I be proud of the culture that was created?"

This is the leadership mirror. It is not always comfortable. It is always clarifying because you cannot shift what you refuse to see.

Personal Note

There was a point in my own leadership where I was moving fast, delivering results, and telling myself I was doing everything "for the team." What I did not realize was that I was also creating urgency everywhere I went. I thought I was being decisive. My team experienced it as pressure.

One day, someone I trusted said to me, gently:

"You know people hold their breath when you walk into a meeting, right?"

That moment stopped me. Not because I was offended — but because I was heartbroken. That was never the experience I wanted for the people working with me.

So, I slowed down. I started naming what I was feeling instead of masking it with speed. I began opening meetings with, "Here is what is on my mind, and here is what I need from you," instead of dumping stress and calling it "urgency."

The dynamic shifted. People started speaking more freely. They looked less guarded. The energy in the room softened.

That experience taught me that self-awareness is not self-criticism. It is self-responsibility.

It is asking, "What is it like to be led by me today?" — and being brave enough to hear the answer.

Leadership Takeaways

- Self-awareness is not a weakness; it is your most significant lever for influence and trust.

- Your presence is never neutral. You are always setting the tone.
- Naming your own state ("I am worried about this timeline") is healthier than acting it out as control.
- Feedback is information, not an attack. Invite it on purpose.
- You cannot ask your team to grow if you are unwilling to grow in front of them.
- Leaders who openly practice self-correction permit their teams to be honest, accountable, and human.

Conclusion: The Leader You Are Shapes the Culture You Create

Skills can make you effective. Self-awareness makes you safe.

When leaders are self-aware, their teams tend to relax. Communication opens. Accountability becomes shared instead of enforced. The work improves because people feel and are more motivated to do it.

Self-awareness also creates credibility. Your team will forgive your mistakes if they trust your honesty. They will not forgive a lack of self-awareness that harms them and goes unacknowledged.

Here is the truth many leaders avoid:

- You are already shaping the culture, whether you mean to or not.
- If you lead with anxiety, you build a culture of tension.
- If you lead with avoidance, you build a culture of silence.
- If you lead with reflection, humility, and a willingness to grow, you build a culture of courage.

Transformation does not begin with changing other people. Transformation starts with the moment you tell the truth about yourself.

Because the most powerful thing you can offer as a leader is not perfection, it is growth that is seen, owned, and modeled in real time. People will follow a leader who is honest about where they are and serious about who they are becoming.

Chapter 11
Leading with Empathy, Vision, and Strategy

"Empathy fuels trust; vision fuels purpose; strategy fuels action." — Veronica Williams

Leading by Example

People often trust actions more than words when it comes to leaders. Demonstrating respect, integrity, and accountability truly helps shape a positive, strong cultural environment.

Balancing Business Goals with Human Needs

Organizations that invest in well-being see higher performance and profitability (Gallup, 2020). Achieving sustainable results is all about practicing in a humane and caring way.

Case Study: Microsoft's Growth Mindset

Satya Nadella's emphasis on curiosity and empathy shifted the culture from internal competition to collaboration—unlocking engagement and innovation.

Vision-Casting and Strategic Alignment

Compelling visions engage hearts and minds. Align strategy and values; translate the mission into role-level ownership and clear goals (Kotter, 6).

Vision Alignment Checklist (Leader Tool)

Does the vision inspire you? Is it shared through stories that resonate, rather than just numbers? Are roles clearly connected to the bigger picture? Does it truly reflect our core values?

Case Study: Patagonia's Values in Action

By aligning their strategy with environmental values—from supply chain to customer engagement—Patagonia has deepened loyalty and added more purpose to their work.

Leadership Takeaway

Begin by understanding others, share a vivid vision, connect your strategy to your core values—and then make it a comforting routine.

Conclusion:

The Future of Work truly puts people first. Leadership plays a crucial role as the heart of driving our organizations toward success and resilience. When organizations focus on creating supportive environments where people feel truly empowered to grow—beyond just focusing on output—employees feel comfortable bringing their genuine selves to work. This openness sparks creativity and teamwork, helping to build a vibrant culture of ongoing learning and development. As a result, talent flourishes, making success sustainable and fulfilling in the long run.

The call to action is inspiring and uplifting: let us come together to create workplaces that truly support and nurture everyone's potential. By doing so, we can ignite a sense of purpose and help each person reach their fullest capabilities. After all, shaping the future of work depends on building spaces where individuals can genuinely become their best selves.

Bonus Materials

Employee Empowerment Toolkit

- Map your strengths vs. current responsibilities
- Self-assess autonomy, recognition, growth, and purpose (1–5)
- Identify one conversation to advance alignment this month

Role Matching Worksheet

List the top 5 strengths and the top 5 energizing tasks; compare with current duties; propose adjustments to close misalignments.

Leadership Reflection Journal Prompts

1) When did a team member last thrive—and why?
2) How does my style change under stress?
3) Which behavior should I model more consistently?

… up to 30 prompts total.

Case Studies from Top-Performing Companies

Google's Project Aristotle highlights psychological safety; Southwest shows that care and humor drive resilience; Unilever's sustainability-focused initiatives build purpose and loyalty (Edmondson, 2019).

Closing Reflection

Leadership is a daily practice. The impact we make is not only measured in outcomes, but in the lives we touch. Take one extra step to listen, support, and connect purpose with action—you will build more than results; you will build a legacy.

— Veronica Williams

About the Author

Veronica has always been fascinated by human nature, and this curiosity has inspired her to pursue a bachelor's degree in psychology, followed by a master's in public administration with a focus on Sustainable Communities. Her journey has led her into leadership roles where she has learned how influential our actions can be—whether it is coaching, mentoring, or fostering environments where others can thrive. Through Williams Evergreen Consultancy, she loves helping leaders and organizations craft cultures where fulfillment blooms beyond just the paycheck.

References

Edmondson, A. C. (2019). The fearless organization: Creating psychological safety in the workplace for learning, innovation, and growth. Wiley.

Gallup. (2020). Employee engagement and performance: Latest insights. Gallup Press.

Goleman, D. (1995). Emotional intelligence: Why it can matter more than IQ. Bantam Books.

Great Place to Work. (n.d.). *Trust vs. engagement: The foundation for retention, innovation, and ROI.* https://www.greatplacetowork.ca/en/articles/trust-vs-engagement-retention-innovation-roi

Kahn, W. A. (1990). Psychological conditions of personal engagement and disengagement at work. Academy of Management Journal, 33(4), 692–724.

Kotter, J. P. (1996). Leading change. Harvard Business School Press.

Maslow, A. H. (1943). A theory of human motivation. Psychological Review, 50(4), 370–396.

Notes

Use this space to capture your reflections, insights, and leadership commitments as you read. What resonated most? What will you put into practice in your workplace?

www.ingramcontent.com/pod-product-compliance
Lightning Source LLC
Chambersburg PA
CBHW071354230926
51846CB00002B/555
9781968151591